Learn Italian

with Nonno

This is my **Nonno**.

This is **Nonno's** kitchen.

He calls it his *cucina*.

Nonno has a fridge in his kitchen.

He puts food in his *frigorifero* to keep it fresh.

There is a freezer too.

What can you see in the **congelatore?**

Did you see the strawberry and chocolate ice cream?

Nonno's favourite is ***gelato alla fragola*** and mine is ***gelato al cioccolato***. Yum!

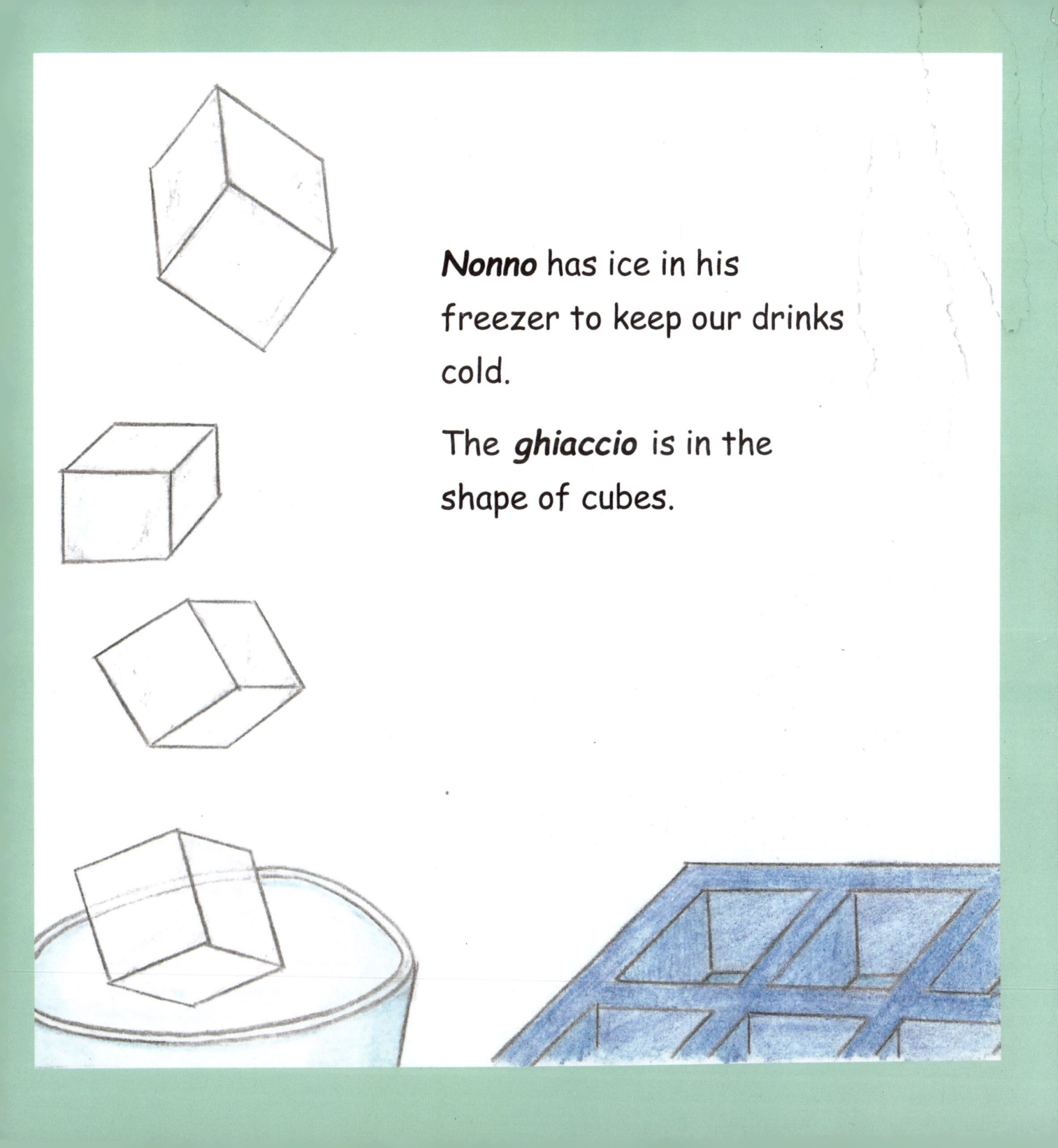

Nonno has ice in his freezer to keep our drinks cold.

The ***ghiaccio*** is in the shape of cubes.

When we want a hot drink **Nonno** uses the **bollitore** to heat water.

Nonno likes **caffè** with **zucchero** and I prefer **tè** with **latte** from the fridge.

There is a **tostapane** to make toast.

Nonno is cooking us **spaghetti al ragù** on the hob. Spaghetti with meat sauce is my favourite!

The bread is nearly ready in the oven.

Look at the delicious *pane* in the *forno!*

It smells *delizioso!*

Can you see the tasty *ragù* and *spaghetti* bubbling away on the *fornello*?

There is a **lavatrice** to wash our clothes when we get them all dirty in **Nonno's** garden.

I like to help **Nonno** with the washing up in the **lavandino**.

I always wash my hands before eating.

The red tap is **calda** and blue tap is **freddo**.

Nonno has a **tavolo** and **sedie** in his kitchen.

I need to put out a plate, knife, fork and glass for **Nonno** and a **piatto**, **coltella**, **forchetta** and **bicchiere** for me too.

Nonno uses salt and pepper when cooking. He sometimes adds **sale** and **pepe** to his food at the table too.

He has a special pepper grinder which is almost as big as me!

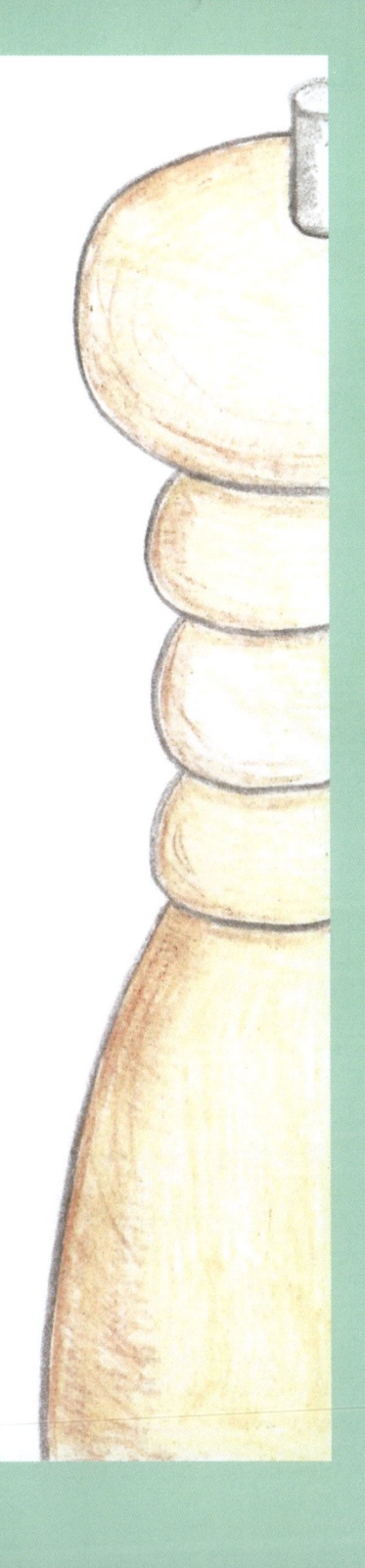

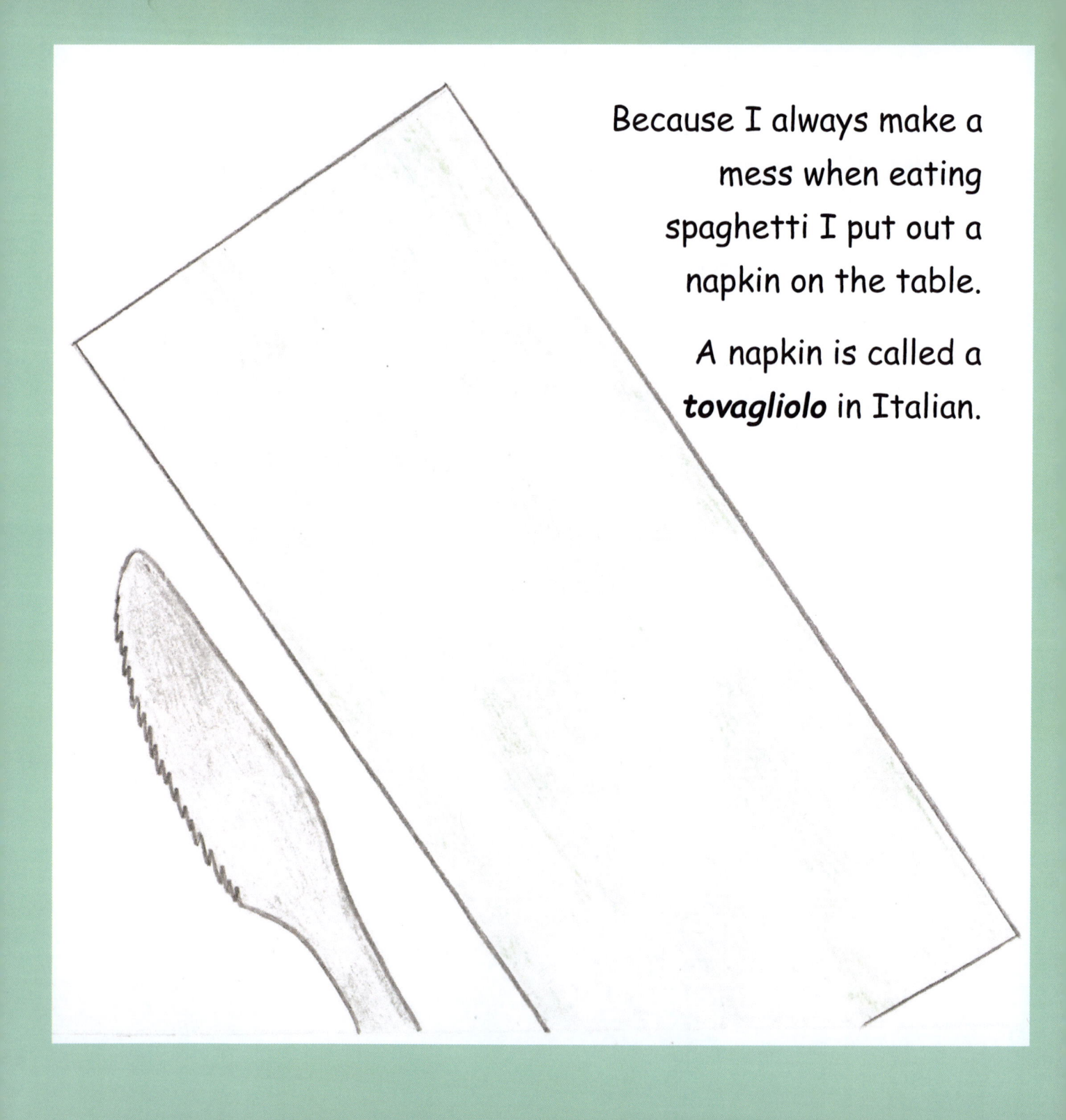

Because I always make a mess when eating spaghetti I put out a napkin on the table.

A napkin is called a **tovagliolo** in Italian.

The **tavolo** is all set for dinner.

How many **forchette** are on the table?

uno...**due!**

There are two forks on the table.
One for **Nonno** and one for me!

Nonno used some *cipollo*, *carota*, *sedano* and garlic to make the *ragù* for our *cena!*

Let's eat dinner! **Mangiare!**

Buon Appetito!

Nonno has taught us some new Italian words

Nonno	**Non**-no	Grandpa
cucina	koo-**chee**-na	kitchen
frigorifero	freego-ree-fayro	fridge
congelatore	konjay-la-**toh**ray	freezer
gelato alla fragola	jay-**lah**to ah-lah **frah**-go-lah	strawberry ice cream
gelato al cioccolato	jay-**lah**to al chok-ko-**lah**ta	chocolate ice cream
ghiaccio	geeat-cho	ice
bollitore	bo-lee-**toh**ray	kettle
caffè	kaf-**fe**	coffee
zucchero	**tsook**-kayro	sugar
tè	te	tea
latte	laht-tay	milk
tostapane	to-**stah**-pahnay	toaster
al ragù	al ra-goo	with meat sauce
pane	pah-nay	bread
forno	for-no	oven
delizioso	day-le-tse'o-zo	delicious
fornello	for-nello	hob/cooker
lavatrice	lava-**tree**chay	washing machine

Nonno has taught us some new Italian words

lavandino	lavan-**dee**-no	sink
caldo	kaldo	hot
freddo	fray-do	cold
tavolo	**tah**-volo	table
sedie	sed-e-ay	chairs
piatto	pee-**at**-to	plate
coltello	kol**tel**-lo	knife
forchetta	for**kayt**-ta	fork
bicchiere	beek-**ye**-ray	glass
sale	sahlay	salt
pepe	paypay	pepper
tovagliolo	taval-**yo**lo	napkin
forchette	for**kayt**-tay	forks
uno	**oo**-no	one
due	**doo**-ay	two
cipolla	chee**pohl**-la	onion
carota	ka-**ro**tah	carrot
sedano	**se**-dano	celery
cena	chay-na	dinner
Mangiare!	mahn-**jah**-ray	Eat!
Buon Appetito!	boo'on ahp-pay-**tee**-to	Enjoy your meal!

The new educational

Learn Italian with Nonno series

Makes an introduction to learning a new language fun for young children.

Each book includes a dictionary with pronunciation for each new word.

Books in series:

Nonno's Garden

Nonno's Kitchen

Nonno's House

Coming soon:

Available in other languages

More adventures with **Nonno**

Printed in Great Britain
by Amazon